★ ★ ★ ★ ★ ★ ★

XTREME RACES
TOUR DE FRANCE

BY S.L. HAMILTON

Visit us at
www.abdopublishing.com

Published by ABDO Publishing Company, PO Box 398166, Minneapolis, MN 55439.
Copyright ©2013 by Abdo Consulting Group, Inc. International copyrights reserved in all countries. No part of this book may be reproduced in any form without written permission from the publisher. A&D Xtreme™ is a trademark and logo of ABDO Publishing Company.

Printed in the United States of America, North Mankato, Minnesota.
112012
012013

Editor: John Hamilton
Graphic Design: Sue Hamilton
Cover Design: John Hamilton
Cover Photos: Getty Images
Interior Photos: AP-pgs 2-3, 8-14, 16, 17, 20-21, 23, 24 (Greg LeMond & Lance Armstrong), 25 (all images except Eddy Merckx), 26-32; Corbis-pg 22; Getty Images-pgs 1, 4-5, 18-19, 25 (Eddy Merckx); Granger Collection-pg 24 (Maurice Garin); Mary Evans-pgs 6-7; Thinkstock-pg 12 (map); Tour de France-pg 15 (map).

ABDO Booklinks
Web sites about Xtreme Races are featured on our Book Links pages. These links are routinely monitored and updated to provide the most current information available.
Web site: www.abdopublishing.com

Cataloging-in-Publication Data

Hamilton, Sue L., 1959-
Tour de France / S.L. Hamilton.
   p. cm. -- (Xtreme races)
Includes index.
ISBN 978-1-61783-697-8
1. Tour de France (Bicycle race)--History--Juvenile literature. 2. Tour de France--Juvenile literature.   I. Title.
796.6--dc23
                        2012946021

TABLE OF CONTENTS

TOUR DE FRANCE

The Tour de France is an extreme bicycle race in which riders battle for about 2,175 grueling miles (3,500 km). For three weeks, racers pedal across France and nearby countries set on winning the world's most famous bicycle race.

XTREME FACT – The Tour de France is also known as "The Big Loop."

HISTORY

The idea for a very long cycling race across France came from Géo Lefèvre, a writer for the sports newspaper *L'Auto*. Editor Henri Desgrange planned the Tour de France hoping interest in the race would help sell more copies of *L'Auto*. Riders started out on July 1, 1903.

The 1903 Tour de France riders depart from Villeneuve-Saint-Georges, a suburb of Paris, France.

People gathered along the route and cheered as the cyclists rode by. Fans bought *L'Auto* to get daily updates. The race was a success! Maurice Garin pedaled to victory in Paris on July 18, 1903. The Tour de France became a yearly event and one of the most popular cycling road races of all time.

XTREME FACT – *Sixty riders entered the 1903 Tour de France, but only 21 actually finished the race.*

TEAMS

Twenty-two teams of nine riders each are invited to compete in the Tour de France. Each team has one leader. The other eight riders, known as *domestiques*, help their leader win. They do this by setting the pace, protecting their leader from hazards, and letting him know when other riders are advancing. Although an individual is named the winner, the win is shared by the entire team.

The BMC Racing Team supports their leader, Cadel Evans, during the 2011 Tour de France. Evans won the race that year.

THE START

The Tour de France begins with the wave of a white flag. Known as the *Grand Départ*, all 198 cyclists start 20 days of racing. Each day, called a "stage," requires about 5 ½ hours of biking. Racers pedal as fast as they can across mountains and plains, and through cities and countryside.

The peloton, the main field of riders, parades through Liege, Belgium, before the start of the 2012 Tour de France.

XTREME FACT – The day before stage one of the Tour de France, each racer competes individually in the Prologue. It is a short, timed race through the starting city. The winner is awarded a yellow jersey to wear the next day at the start of the Tour de France.

THE COURSE

The Tour de France course changes each year, although it always ends in Paris. The route takes riders across France, and often into neighboring countries, such as Spain, Italy, Switzerland, Belgium, Germany, Luxembourg, and the United Kingdom. In total, riders will pedal across about 2,175 miles (3,500 km) of countryside.

XTREME FACT – Tour de France racers receive two rest days over the three-week period.

THE STAGES

Tour de France stages are either flat, hilly, or mountainous. Lengths of each stage vary. Every stage has a winner. Points are awarded to the winner, as well as the first 15 riders across the halfway point and the stage's finish line. There are also individual time-trial days, similar to the Prologue, where riders receive points for finishing the quickest.

Tejay van Garderen races in an individual time-trial on the 19th stage of the 2012 Tour de France.

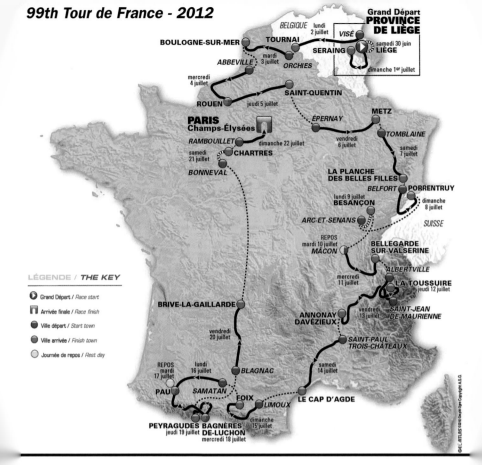

99th Tour de France - 2012

BELGIQUE
Grand Départ
PROVINCE DE LIÈGE
lundi 2 juillet
VISÉ
samedi 30 juin
BOULOGNE-SUR-MER
TOURNAI
SERAING
LIÈGE
dimanche 1er juillet
ABBEVILLE
mardi 3 juillet
ORCHIES
mercredi 4 juillet
SAINT-QUENTIN
ROUEN
jeudi 5 juillet
METZ
ÉPERNAY
TOMBLAINE
vendredi 6 juillet
samedi 7 juillet
PARIS
Champs-Élysées
RAMBOUILLET
dimanche 22 juillet
LA PLANCHE DES BELLES FILLES
samedi 21 juillet
CHARTRES
BELFORT
PORRENTRUY
BONNEVAL
lundi 9 juillet
BESANÇON
dimanche 8 juillet
ARC-ET-SENANS
SUISSE
REPOS
mardi 10 juillet
MÂCON
BELLEGARDE SUR-VALSERINE
ALBERTVILLE
mercredi 11 juillet
LA TOUSSUIRE
jeudi 12 juillet
BRIVE-LA-GAILLARDE
ANNONAY DAVÉZIEUX
vendredi 13 juillet
SAINT-JEAN DE-MAURIENNE
vendredi 20 juillet
SAINT-PAUL TROIS-CHÂTEAUX
REPOS
mardi 17 juillet
lundi 16 juillet
BLAGNAC
samedi 14 juillet
PAU
SAMATAN
FOIX
LIMOUX
LE CAP D'AGDE
PEYRAGUDES
BAGNÈRES
jeudi 19 juillet
DE-LUCHON
mercredi 18 juillet
dimanche 15 juillet

LÉGENDE / THE KEY

- Grand Départ / Race start
- Arrivée finale / Race finish
- Ville départ / Start town
- Ville arrivée / Finish town
- Journée de repos / Rest day

STAGE		DATE	LOCATION	LENGTH	
Prologue		June 30	Liège > Liège	6.4 km	(4 miles)
1	Flat	July 1	Liège > Seraing	198 km	(123 m)
2	Flat	July 2	Visé > Tournai	207.5 km	(129 m)
3	Hilly	July 3	Orchies > Boulogne-sur-Mer	197 km	(122 m)
4	Flat	July 4	Abbeville > Rouen	214.5 km	(133 m)
5	Flat	July 5	Rouen > Saint-Quentin	196.5 km	(122 m)
6	Flat	July 6	Épernay > Metz	205 km	(127 m)
7	Hilly	July 7	Tomblaine > La Planche des Belles Filles	199 km	(124 m)
8	Hilly	July 8	Belfort > Porrentruy	157.5 km	(98 m)
9	Time-Trial	July 9	Arc-et-Senans > Besançon	41.5 km	(26 m)
-	Rest day	July 10	Repos		
10	Mountain	July 11	Mâcon > Bellegarde-sur-Valserine	194.5 km	(121 m)
11	Mountain	July 12	Albertville > La Toussuire - Les Sybelles	148 km	(92 m)
12	Hilly	July 13	Saint-Jean-de-Maurienne > Annonay Davézieux	226 km	(140 m)
13	Flat	July 14	Saint-Paul-Trois-Châteaux > Le Cap d'Agde	217 km	(135 m)
14	Mountain	July 15	Limoux > Foix	191 km	(119 m)
15	Flat	July 16	Samatan > Pau	158.5 km	(99 m)
-	Rest day	July 17	Repos		
16	Mountain	July 18	Pau > Bagnères-de-Luchon	197 km	(122 m)
17	Mountain	July 19	Bagnères-de-Luchon > Peyragudes	143.5 km	(89 m)
18	Flat	July 20	Blagnac > Brive-la-Gaillarde	222.5 km	(138 m)
19	Time-Trial	July 21	Bonneval > Chartres	53.5 km	(33 m)
20	Flat	July 22	Rambouillet > Paris Champs-Élysées	120 km	(75 m)

Riders may finish a stage in one town, and then be driven to another location (see dotted lines on the map) to start another stage the next day.

THE JERSEYS

Colored jerseys and prize money are awarded to point winners at the end of each stage of the race.

- Yellow Jersey - General Classification
- Green Jersey - Points Classification
- Red Polka Dot Jersey - Best Climber Classification
- White Jersey - Best Young Rider

Yellow jersey winners are awarded to the leader who has completed all the preceding stages in the least amount of time. Every Tour de France racer wants to "wear yellow," even for just one stage. The ultimate Tour de France winner is awarded the yellow jersey.

Bradley Wiggins wins the yellow jersey during the 2012 Tour de France.

16

Peter Sagan

The green jersey goes to the racer with the most sprint points. Racers earn sprint points by going as fast as they can in certain sections of each stage. The most points are awarded during flat stages where riders can go all out. Fast sprinters try to win the green jersey.

Jérôme Pineau

The red polka dot jersey goes to the "King of the Mountains." It is awarded to the fastest climber to the top of a slope. Racers are given points based on the difficulty of the climb. The most difficult climb up a tall mountain gives the winner 20 points.

Thomas Löfkvist

The white jersey is awarded to the best young rider who is 25 years old or less. Similar to the leader's yellow jersey, the white jersey is awarded to the young racer with the fastest individual time, combining each preceding stage's time.

THE RULES

There are many detailed rules for Tour de France racers.

One important rule is that racers must wear a bike helmet. They must also dress in their team uniform and wear their team number. Racers must pass drug tests before, during, and after the race.

Jan Ullrich takes a food bag in the feed zone during the 2005 Tour de France. Racers eat 5,000-6,000 calories a day, about three times more than an average person!

Team vehicles, which carry spare bikes, water, food, and medical supplies, must drive in the order assigned. Racers are handed food and water bags in the "feed zone." They eat and drink as they ride.

STRATEGY TO WIN

Tour de France racers are at their peak in strength and endurance. Racers practice on the course for weeks before the race, sometimes even months and years beforehand.

XTREME FACT – The longest Tour de France was held in 1926. The race was 3,569 miles (5,745 km) long.

A major strategy is to use the peloton, or main group of riders, to the best advantage. Riding in a group allows a racer to draft. Drafting is to ride very closely behind another person to benefit from reduced wind resistance. Racers must know when to take advantage of the peloton and when to break away and race ahead.

The peloton rides together near Montgardin in southeastern France during the 2006 Tour de France.

DANGERS

Tour de France riders race at twice the speed of an average cyclist. Bad things can happen fast. There have been collisions between racers, between riders and fans, and with Tour vehicles. Usually, there are only injuries. However, from 2000-2009, three fans were killed after stepping in front of Tour vehicles.

Racers collide in the 2003 Tour de France. Racers did not yet have to wear helmets.

Racer Johnny Hoogerland collided with a media car during the 2011 Tour de France. The cyclist rolled down a hill and into a barbed wire fence. Hoogerland finished the race with many injuries.

Three cyclists to date have died while racing in the Tour. Francisco Cepeda died in 1935 after losing control while speeding down a mountain. Tom Simpson had a fatal heart attack in 1967. Drugs were later found in his system. In 1995, Fabio Casartelli fell and struck his head on a concrete block. His death made clear the need for helmets.

Famous Cyclists

The Tour de France is a grueling, three-week test of focus, strength, and determination. A few cyclists have become famous Tour racers.

First Winner

Maurice Garin won the first 1903 Tour de France. His time over six stages was 94 hours, 33 minutes, 14 seconds.

First American Winner

Greg LeMond is the first American to win the Tour de France. He won in 1986, 1989, and 1990.

Most Well-Known Racer

American Lance Armstrong was awarded Tour de France wins in 1999, 2000, 2001, 2002, 2003, 2004, and 2005. He was stripped of his wins in 2012 for drug use (doping). Officials have decided that those years will have no official winner.

Most Wins

Four racers have won the Tour de France five times to date.

Jacques Anquetil of France won in 1957, 1961, 1962, 1963, and 1964.

Eddy Merckx of Belgium won in 1969, 1970, 1971, 1972, and 1974

Bernard Hinault of France won in 1978, 1979, 1981, 1982 and 1985.

Miguel Indurain of Spain won in 1991, 1992, 1993, 1994, and 1995.

Sprint Points Winner

Erik Zabel of Germany finished with the most sprint points in six Tour de France races. He won the green jersey in 1996, 1997, 1998, 1999, 2000, and 2001.

King of the Mountains

Richard Virenque of France is the Tour de France record holder as King of the Mountains. He won the award seven times: 1994, 1995, 1996, 1997, 1999, 2003, and 2004.

TRADITIONS

Since its start in 1903, the Tour de France has been held annually, except during the years of World War I and II. A number of traditions have formed over the course of nearly 100 Tours.

Fabian Cancellara proudly wears the overall leader's yellow jersey after winning the second stage of the 2012 Tour de France.

The most well-known Tour de France tradition began in 1919. That year, stage-11 winner Eugène Christophe was asked to wear a yellow jersey. The yellow made the leader stand out. Some say yellow was chosen because the sponsoring newspaper, L'Auto, was printed on yellow paper. Others say it was because no one else wore yellow. At first, riders did not like the attention they received. Canary calls rang out from teasing fans. Over time, that stopped. Today, every racer is proud to "wear yellow."

Cadel Evans stopped with a flat tire during the 14th stage of the 2012 Tour de France.

Bradley Wiggins (yellow jersey) slowed the peloton until Cadel Evans could catch up. Bradley Wiggins went on to win the 2012 Tour de France.

Cadel Evans

Bradley Wiggins

The Tour de France is a race of honor. When a leader has a flat tire or his bike breaks down, it is a tradition for the other leaders to slow down the rest of the peloton until the racer is back in his original spot. Then the race is on again.

Winners of each stage of the Tour de France are awarded flowers and a plush lion. Many people think the lion stands for the racers's fierceness. In fact, the lion is the logo of the French bank Credit Lyonnaise. The bank has sponsored the race since 1987.

THE FINISH

After three weeks of racing, the winner sprints to the finish on the Avenue des Champs-Élysées in Paris, France. Winners in all classifications are awarded their trophies on this famous street.

Bradley Wiggins (yellow jersey) is congratulated by teammate Michael Rogers. Wiggins became the 2012 Tour de France winner and the first Tour winner from Great Britain.

The 99th Tour de France winner Bradley Wiggins stands in front of Paris's Arc de Triomphe (Arch of Triumph).

Le Tour de France 2012

Bradley Wiggins gives a kiss to his 2012 Tour de France trophy. It is a ceramic bowl made by Manufacture Nationale de Sèvres.

Prize money is awarded to all the winners in all the classifications. The Tour winner receives a hefty paycheck of about $550,000!

GLOSSARY

DOMESTIQUES
The eight members of a Tour de France team who help their leader win. In French, the word means "servants."

DOPING
To illegally use a drug that improves an athlete's performance.

DRAFTING
When one racer takes the lead and others ride closely behind him. This shelters the non-leading riders as less effort is needed to maintain the same pace. However, it is against the rules for racers to draft behind vehicles.

GRAND DÉPART
The first stage of the Tour de France when all 198 riders begin the race.

KING OF THE MOUNTAINS
The best climber in a mountain stage. The red polka dot jersey is awarded to the King of the Mountains winner.

PELOTON

The main group of riders.

PROLOGUE

The individual time-trial race held before the start of the Tour de France's stage one. The winner of the Prologue wears the yellow jersey during stage one.

ROAD RACE

In cycling, a race held on paved roads. The Tour de France is one of the longest and most well-known road races.

SPRINT

To race at very high speeds for a short period of time. In cycling, a racer will often sprint to the finish, trying to make up some time and win the race. In the Tour de France, the best sprinter is awarded the green jersey.

INDEX